Behind the Mask

Bari Rolfe

Copyright © Bari Rolfe, 1977.
Copyright Renewed © by the Estate of Bari Rolfe, 2011.
All rights reserved, including the right to reproduction in whole or in part.

OTHER WORKS BY THE AUTHOR
    Actions Speak Louder: A Workbook for Actors*
    Commedia dell'Arte, A Scene Study Book*
    Behind the Mask*
    Mime Directory "Bibliography" (editor)
    Mimes on Miming (anthology)
   * *Available from Charlemagne Press*

Library and Archives Canada Cataloguing in Publication

Rolfe, Bari
    Behind the mask / Bari Rolfe.

Includes bibliographical references.
ISBN 978-0-921845-36-2

    1. Masks. 2. Acting. I. Title.

PN2071.M37R65 2011   792.02'8   C2011-906034

Charlemagne Press
4348 Coastview Drive
Garden Bay, BC
V0N 1S1 Canada

CONTENTS

Foreword, 1

Preface, 3

Mask: Affect and Effect, 9

Universal Mask, 21

Character Mask, 33

Countermask, 41

Half Mask, 45

Tai Chi Ch'uan and the Universal Mask, 49

Mime and Mask as Rehearsal Aids, 55

Bibliography, 59

Photographs, 65

To Marcel Marceau,
who first showed me the poetic world of
movement

My thanks go primarily to Jacques Lecoq, master teacher who opened many doors and invited me to walk through. Lawrence Fixel was unfailingly willing to listen and to talk. Susan Suchman and Leonard Pitt made valuable suggestions. I also thank all the other "mask freaks," students and colleagues, who shared experiences with me.

The reader will find the words "he," "him," and "his" used generically when I found it unavoidable. "Actor" refers to players of both sexes.

FOREWORD

This book is addressed first to actors and their needs for expressive bodies, ability to play in heroic dimensions, simplicity and economy in movement, and freedom in assuming roles.

Masks, though, can offer everyone a certain self-knowledge; through a false face one can find a true face.

Masks are not an end in themselves, but simply a learning tool for anyone who responds to them, and for actors who most of the time will play without masks. The benefits of mask work can be achieved without an actual mask, by letting the face become the mask, but the physical object, through its associations with metamorphosis, magic, and identification, make the way infinitely easier.

The old comedy had used masks, but the new comedy played bareface till one Roscius Gallus, the most excellent player among the Romanes brought up these vizards which we see at this day used partly to supply the want of players, when there were more parts than there were persons, or that it was not thought meet to trouble and pester princes' chambers with too many folkes. Now by the chaunge of a vizard one man might play the king and carter, the old nurse and the young damsell, the marchant and the souldier or any other part he listed very conveniently.
  -George Puttenham,
  The Arte of English Poesie

PREFACE

per•son•na [Latin *persona*, mask, PERSON]
(a)person / mask / person(a)
person / mask / role

A mask is a role: many faces, many facets.

A mask effaces who we are, to show who we want to be.

A mask hides, and reveals that which it hides.

A mask is oneself, the realization of the inner spirit, and
A mask is the "other": person, animal, god . . .

A mask can be voluntary, and
A mask can be involuntary.

A mask can aid communication, and
A mask can hinder communication.

A mask permits all, and
A mask imprisons in the fixed role.

A mask confers immortality, and
A mask confers death.

A mask offers solitude, and
A mask offers participation.

A mask is a medium of truth, for even when it is meant to lie, its very use to hide or cover reveals the subterfuge.

A mask is a link with what we cannot otherwise touch: the spirit of the god, the dead, the other.

A mask is the instrument of metamorphosis, a way to reach the powers to which it appeals; the wearer is the channel to the god, then becomes the channel through which its response is passed to the members of the tribe.

If the body is dull, if the mind is dull, the mask is meaningless.

The mask which an actor wears is apt to become his face.
— Plato

We adopt the mask, live with the mask, and finally become the mask.
— Paul Valery

Masks cannot be put on or taken off in public, since putting on a mask turns a person into a spirit, and lends him supernatural qualities.
— *Masked Rituals of the Afikpo*

The artist flows into the mask the poet offers him; only so will the god possess him.
— Mary Renault

Masks are dreams caught and fixed.
> – Georges Buraud

I wonder if a mask, being universal, enhances our relations with others more than does the naked face?
> – Kobo Abe

"Persona" also means "character"; "character" and "stage personage" have often been synonymous. In effect, one is or one has a character only in relation to others, one shows it, represents it. It is a kind of mask, but it also what we are.
> – Alessandro Pizzorno

Behind the Mask

MASK: AFFECT AND EFFECT

A function of theatre is the participation in the existence of other beings . . . . to recognize oneself. This is delegated in our society to the actor.
— Alessandro Pizzorno

The theatre's twin masks of comedy and tragedy originated as the representations of Dionysus, father of drama, god of wine, and patron deity of Greek drama festivals. The linking of comedy and tragedy in one god is typical of the paradoxes and dualities that surround Dionysus and the mask, both symbols of drama. For one, there is his own double theatre mask. Then, unlike other deities, he was a god who came down from Olympus and moved among mortal men. Also, the mask is a man-made object, yet it inspires fear and exaltation — as though it was beyond mortal touch. It is presence and absence. It is death and life. The mask is a complete object in itself, but it lacks a reverse side; thus it invites a living participant to wear and thereby complete it. And much more.

Masks have long been associated with theatre as it emerged from ritual, from sympathetic magic, from religion, from

shamanism, from festivals, from totems. Greek tragedy
and then comedic farce used the mask, as did Chinese,
Japanese, and other Asian theatre. In the 16th century the
Commedia dell'arte characters were as unchanging as
the masks they bore. Recently there has been a revival of
the use of masks in more contemporary theatre. Gordon
Craig sparked interest, especially in Commedia dell'arte,
through his stage work and in a periodical he called,
appropriately enough, *The Mask*, 1908-1929. In 1923
Kenneth Macgowan saw a spirit of religion calling the
mask back to the stage. Playwrights Eugene O'Neill and
W. B. Yeats responded to its theatricality and used masks in
their plays in the early 1900's. Literal or figurative masked
characters populated the plays of Jean Genet, Claude van
Itallie, John Arden, Michel de Ghelderode, Bertoldt Brecht
in the 1950's and 1960's, and in most of the current street,
action and radical theatres like Bread and Puppet Theatre
in New York, the San Francisco Mime Troupe, El Teatro
Campesino and Epic West on the West Coast. We also see
certain stage productions in which the director employs
masks, even though the playwright did not call for them.
So masks, both as symbol and in practice, have been part of
theatre since its beginnings.

But what happens *behind* the mask? What effect does
it have on the actor? The impact of mask, not upon the
spectator but on the actor, has been very little examined,
and its use as a training technique and rehearsal tool is
not widely known or understood. Masks were not used in
European acting training until the early 1920's, beginning
with Jacques Copeau at the Vieux Colombier in Paris, and
in America much later than that.[1] Jean Dorcy, who studied

---

* See Sears Eldridge's documentation, 1975, listed in bibliography with Copeau and who has written extensively on mime and theatre, recounts that important circumstance too briefly in *J'Aime la Mime*: "By the intuition of genius Copeau, who seemed to us to be still very close to childhood games, encouraged our bents and let us invent and develop our little dramas. In the depths of that laboratory the mask was born." From their experiences, specific uses of the mask as a part of actor training were then developed; they found that it helped the actors to use their bodies more expressively, to eliminate any unconscious physical mannerisms which could hamper them, and to reach a simple, broad, objective style of play. Mask work helped prepare actors for classical acting or for tragedy, and enabled them to participate in the desired style of a given production. Michel Saint-Denis, who belonged to the school of Copeau and who later established some of the world's most prestigious acting schools, summarizes the purpose and the effect of the mask in *Theatre, The Rediscovery of Style*:

> *To us, a mask was a temporary instrument which we offered to the curiosity of the young actor, in the hope that it might help his concentration, strengthen his inner feelings, diminish his self-consciousness, and help him to develop his powers of outward expression.*

He describes some of the effect of the mask as demanding of the actor only controlled, strong and utterly simple actions; it brings about the desired state of warm heart with cool head; it absorbs the actor's personality while at the same time only the actor can bring a mask to life.

Perhaps the role of the mask in primitive religion, shamanism, and ancient drama unconsciously affects our reactions to the mask today, but such a discussion is beyond the scope of this work. Instead, we turn our attention to *how* the mask works for the actor, rather than why it works.

The most important factor in the effectiveness of the mask is the impulse to identify physically with it, that is, to assume its outer form. The identification can be conscious or not. On putting on a mask, the actor often feels that his own features, hidden behind the mask, are drawn into a semblance of its traits. One smiles with its smile, one frowns with its frown. The identification extends to the body, for with one's own face arranged in a particular way, the body too feels an impulse to complete the identification. A pinched face might call forth a contraction in the chest; a noble facial aspect might lift the head and ribcage. So the body is drawn into posture and gesture which harmonize with the actual face, which is identifying with the mask face.

This total configuration of the person, the face and body in harmony with the mask, is a key element in the training process. A body that can respond to various masks is an expressive body. A body that can unself-consciously give itself to the total identification, with total commitment, is capable of range, sensitivity, and theatrical dimension.

Something else of great importance also occurs: the physical configuration of the body creates a pathway into the interior of a characterization suggested by the mask. Makeup, acting as a mask, can have a similar effect. Michael Chekhov, director and teacher, advises the actor to put on a face as though it were makeup. "The more you can imagine your face as resembling that of the person you have under scrutiny," he said in *To the Director and Playwright*, "the more will you be able to experience what this person experiences. For by thus penetrating his psychology, you open the door to a truer knowledge of his inner life." The Kabuki actor studies himself in costume and makeup for a time before making his entrance, for "one feels like the bamboo when one looks at the bamboo." The principle of identification and its attendant evoking of the psyche is not a new phenomenon, and extends beyond theatre. An English psychologist imitated her patients' gestures and postures as a means of realizing their states of mind; she made herself receptive and suggestible, and applied the motor-ideo (from the motion to its motivating idea) type of imitation to bring herself closer to them. And in *Literature As Experience*, Bacon and Breen observe that to learn something about an object, animate or inanimate, it is necessary to assume the attitude [form] of the object.

In studying tribal rituals, anthropologists have noted that masks can confer a sense of freedom upon the wearer, that the concealment of one's own identity permits one an added freedom. Margaret Mead, in her study *Masks and Man*, found that "those who wear the masks are able to assume new roles, to move with a license or a dignity, a ferocity or a frozen grace unattainable without a mask."

The mask helps the actor too to assume new roles and to move in ways appropriate to the role; the mask gives him added impetus, and he is free to go further in the direction suggested by the mask, to make larger choices. He also feels a freedom from inhibition and self-consciousness – perhaps a kind of courage – and freedom from the limitations of habitual ways of moving and reacting, so that something quite different, even unexpected, can filter through the body and stand revealed.

Because the mask confers freedom it is safe; it is an object to hide behind physically, and a characterization to hide behind emotionally. But the mask both hides and reveals. When the face is hidden the wearer feels entirely hidden – something of an ostrich effect – so the body is left free to respond expressively, unself-consciously. In this way the mask can act as a medium through which both strengths and weaknesses of the actor can be seen. An actor can don a mask, assume its dimension, and achieve an unsuspected presence and power, unknown even to himself. On the other hand, it is a valuable corrective in that it reveals pitilessly any faults or inadequacies in stance or movement. Minor posture problems or ineffective choices of movement, usually not noticeable, become glaringly obvious. The slightest droop in the chest, or tension in a shoulder, is magnified and seems suddenly to spring into view. The mask, dramatic in itself, throws into relief anything around it, making it appear larger than life if it is consistent with the mask, and overtly incongruous if it is not. Yet in spite of the revelation flowing from the mask, the safety and protection it offers remain intact and are not compromised.

A first lesson the actor learns is to get out of the way, as it were, to let him or herself be influenced by the mask; not to impose anything upon it but instead to be receptive to it. Getting out of the way means simply doing nothing at first, nothing of one's own habits of walking, standing, sitting, gesturing. A state of receptivity, of being available, is thereby created, an empty, fallow place where something can come from the mask to the wearer. As some students observed, it almost leads one by the hand!

The effect of the mask is predicated upon a separation from the imprint of the actor's personality and from the wearer's daily life. An actor without technique can often be effective on personality alone; in a mask that would not be possible because one is imposing one's own personality upon the mask – an imposition it resists. Learning this lesson from the mask is learning that one can be expressive with the body alone, without the use of face or voice. Even when a particular mask utilizes elements of the wearer's personality, which it inevitably does, the actor's naturalistic movements and habitual gestures of real life present an incongruity, an inconsistency with the mask; it calls, rather, for movement larger than life, more important than minor or trivial actions. One cannot simply don a mask and go about one's ordinary business.

The separation from daily life cannot take place under such circumstances. The mask does become, should become, a sacred object; in it the actor feels a sense of magic, of grandeur and of mystery, too often lost in the slick, commercial shuffle and the wise-cracking exchange of the theatre.

How does a mask help to make the torso and its movements more expressive? With the face hidden and the voice stilled – the two most expressive features of the actor's means – there is only one way for the performer to express anything: through the body and its movements. "If the face is hidden, the actor's body becomes a whole face, expressing at a distance what the real face expresses close up," said French writer Jean Cocteau. A director of Britain's Royal Ballet commented, "Some critics have complained that one or two of these dancers have tremendous technique but lack personality when they dance at Covent Garden. But that changes; something wonderful happens to the same performers when they put on masks ... Facial immobility somehow forced an increase in balletic expression. The characters [in the ballet *Peter Rabbit*] had to act with their whole bodies, not just from the neck up. It gave everything a marvelous simplicity, and a sense of stylistic unity."

It is also a quality of mask that it fills time and space. Cocteau, above, spoke of the effective distance of the whole body-become-face. Masks seems to invest the space around them with their presence, to charge the surrounding air with importance. Also, distance is needed in order to see the entire figure – a long shot rather than a closeup. Time too is charged; the mask requires a tempo different from that of daily life, and is highly effective with moments of immobility. The actor, accepting the mask's investing of each gesture with importance, tends to eliminate nonessential movement; those that remain are thus clearer, simpler, and perhaps even enlarged or made minuscule, both of which dimensions are well supported by the mask.

Less equals more.

The principle of less equals more enforces an economy of movement, valuable for an actor to learn. At first one wants to compensate for the seeming static features of a mask by busy movement, not yet realizing that one should move less in order to let the mask "move" – or rather, become alive, not necessarily in motion but simply in its place on a live, sensitive body. Stillness helps, for the mask gives great presence. But even that presumed stasis of a mask is only a seeming immobility, for masks appear to change expression, a phenomenon noted in every group's experience. Some of this is due to viewing angle; looking at a mask from a high or low point (chin lowered or chin lifted), or in three-quarter view or profile, often produces differing expressions. Sometimes changes of light will throw shadows that suggest moving "facial" features. Most frequently, however, the reason for the mask seeming to move is that we "read" into its face those expressions that we actually see in the body. A smiling mask can suddenly look pathetic if the actor's chest droops slightly; the upturned mouth becomes fearful and tremulous. The Indian dancer Rajkumar Suddenhendra observed that "expression does not flow from my face to my body, but is transmitted from my body to my face."

The sensitive actor approaches a mask, first by simply looking at it; here the identification begins. When he places the mask he remains still, emptying himself: his mind of plans, his body of customary rhythms and movements. He even empties his lungs of air so that something different can come to him with a fresh breath. He observes himself in a mirror, letting the identification pervade his body. He becomes immersed in it, then gradually searches for appropriate posture, walk, small gestures. A fusion of person and mask takes place that brings the Latin word persona (mask) round full circle. When that fusion is achieved, he feels a sense of simplicity plus authority; he can "carry" the mask. The experience of Mary Wigman, innovator of modern dance in Germany in the 1930's, corroborates this. In *The Language of Dance* she counsels that dancers, to achieve deep identification with a mask, contemplate it, observe themselves in mirrors, then slowly give the body the gait, posture, gesture of the mask.

The mystique of the mask is powerful. One immediately feels different behind it. When an actor is responding to the commands of the mask, he experiences a sense of wholeness, relaxation, and well-being. There is a calm sensation of being taken over by it. If he is improvising he finds himself doing unexpected things, feeling impelled to obey the choices suggested by the mask.

Its theatrical mystique has led to associated rituals. The Greek and Roman actors undertook a long, silent communion with their masks before putting them on; there are a number of reliefs depicting such a scene, thus indicating its importance. There is a current ritual in the Noh theatre: a box containing the masks of the two merry old men is carried on stage. When the actor taking the traditional role of Okina enters, he bows low before the audience. The mask is taken out of the box and placed upon his face. After he has given his slow and dignified dance, the mask is taken off and put back with great respect. The humorous dance of Sanbaso is next given with the same procedure.

In Copeau's school students donned the mask; the French terms are *"coiffer,"* to put on a hat, or *"chausser,"* to put on shoes, words that suggest the intimate harmony between mask and wearer. They treated the mask with much respect, almost ritualistically, as they held it in the left hand, looked at it for a time, then fitted it over the face while the right hand adjusted the elastic – all to be done in one gesture, and all preparatory to performing the exercises. In this way they kept freshly before them the importance of that object, and entered into a receptive state of mind and body.

Whether or not one performs a rite, actors can be encouraged, as they watch others work, to hold a mask and let their hands become familiar with its features and textures; they should refrain from treating the mask casually, holding it or swinging it by its elastic. Once masked, they accept being under its influence; if it is necessary to clarify any questions, they lift the mask in order to speak. This sets up firmly the convention of being someone else whenever the mask is in place. In rehearsal, once a scene is stopped and the actors must talk, the mask is slipped to the top of the head and worn there for the necessary time. These conventions help to create the circumstances for the most effective work.

Actors are not the only artists to note the effect of masks. Playwright John Arden discovered that the actor in a mask cannot behave as though he were not wearing it. He also found an effect on his writing, that it demanded simple, pared-down language as it does simple, pared-down gesture; and that the mask is so powerful in itself that it needs what he called a more naked expression of emotion. Mary Wigman found that she could not move contrary to what the mask "decreed," that she could not impose movement upon the mask but had to listen to its requirements. Eugene O'Neill watched rehearsals of his *Great God Brown*, a play done in masks, and commented that it was interesting to see how, after using their masks for a time, the actors reacted to the demand made by the masks that their bodies become alive and expressive. He observed that, once mastered, its lessons were retained by the body and the mind even when masks were not worn. O'Neill also anticipated certain fears on the part of actors, fears which actually are expressed at times: that masks will depersonalize them and will deprive them of the very important element of facial play. His response is that, on the contrary, actors in masks would explore many undeveloped possibilities of expression, and "after all, masks did not extinguish the Greek actor, nor have they kept the action of the Asian theatre from being an art." The fears are groundless, for whether used for performance or for training, the mask can offer self-knowledge, enlargement, objectivity, and profoundly moving experiences.

o o o

The next sections deal with certain specific types of masks. Teachers of mask work use a variety of kinds of masks. The dissertation by Sears Eldredge, referred to earlier, describes in detail several schools of mask teaching in the United States.

UNIVERSAL MASK

The wearer of the mask . . . is himself and yet someone else. Madness has touched him . . . something of the mystery . . . which resides in masks, and whose last descendant is the actor.
— Walter Otto

The universal mask is an inner one. It represents that which human beings have in common, without the reactions and attitudes with which individuals relate to the world. We start from birth, or before, to cope in our various ways; those ways become our personalities, individual and unique. But at each person's center remains an inner core of what we share with all humankind – the same senses, physiology, and survival needs. We all relate to objects and situations around us, and the purpose of the universal mask is to help us determine the simplest, minimal way to deal with them, to do only that which is required by the object or situation itself with nothing extra added, extra being gestures or energy not needed to handle the object or respond to the situation. For example, the action of shoveling requires certain actions: thrust, lever, lift, throw.

An individual may wipe the brow, hitch trousers, lean on the shovel, but none of these are required to perform the act of shoveling.

Neutral mask, *le masque neutre*, is the name it bears in France. Unfortunately, the adjective in English has somewhat pejorative associations; no one wants to be neutral, which is equated with being nothing, and the negative association can interfere with work in the mask. The term "universal" is appropriate, as the word is embodied in the description of this mask, that it represents what we all have in common.

In looking for the universal reaction to a given moment, we learn how we reveal our own personality or character reactions which differ from the universal. Such self-knowledge is important, for with it actors can choose to include or omit personal characteristics from a future role. A truly universal individual does not exist – no one can be humankind ("I've never SEEN mankind!"). So with the universal mask one searches not for a person but for universal reactions to the things in the world. One determines what actions or movements are required by an object itself, a situation itself. Now, in dealing with the specific moves, the word "neutral" is useful to describe an act, for everyone does engage in neutral movements, gestures, tones of voice, rhythms. This is especially true of work and sport motions, for when they are done efficiently, the movements are neutral; that is, they are essential (necessary), and economical, and these two words together can define the universal. The universal reaction is one that is essential to execute the given task, what everyone would have to do, and an execution that is done with economy of gesture. Most of the sorting out in the mask revolves around finding out what is essential, for life-long habits intrude at first. If an athlete kept rubbing or touching his nose (to choose a gesture that is very common, almost "universal," among young actors), that movement would be unnecessary and inappropriate to the act of diving, or other sport activities.

One can begin by imagining a simple, ordinary situation, say, to pick up a stone; then to think of executing only that which must be done in order to accomplish it, reacting to the thing itself, in the present, with no past recalled (it's not heavier than you remembered) and no future anticipated (it won't bite). What one does, therefore, is what everyone would need to do in the same circumstances. A useful phrase is this: "listening to the other." The "other" is whatever one is relating to; the stone by its size and weight "tells" one what to do and how to do it. The necessity, and joy, of listening to the other is dramatically evident in watching someone skiing, or on a skateboard, a trampoline, with a ball in motion, or handling an object. The body bends, leans, reaches, absorbs impact, gathers its forces, entirely in response to the objects and circumstances. More: fabrics by their weave and weight tell one how best to fashion them; the text of a play, music for dancing, the words on the page one is writing – all these have inherent, integral requirements that tell the person dealing with them precisely what to do. Peter Schumann, describing the handling of rod puppets for his Bread and Puppet Theatre, states that the "operator has to learn to be a translator, to not so much be interested in his own dancing body, but rather in fabrics and materials that he has to learn the weight of and the speed that's possible with that weight, and the expressions that go along with it." In the same way the universal mask lets one respond to the thing itself, free of subjective elements that might affect the "listening to the other."

Neutral can also be thought of as zero, a point of departure for measuring movement in time, in space, and with energy. "He was agitated" or "he was lethargic" assumes the existence of a state of non-agitation, non-lethargy, a kind of zero point from which to evaluate variations of energy levels. That assumption is an unconscius pegging of the zero point, which we all do all the time; awareness is revealed in the very comment "he was agitated," for we are measuring the state of being from an assumed zero point of non-agitation. To be aware of a neutral point of departure helps to sharpen our sensitivity to variations, even the most subtle. With practice.

To find what is neutral, we often describe what it is not. A neutral walk is neither fast nor slow, neutral stance is neither slumped nor stiff. Sometimes we know what is not neutral when an act gives rise to a question: if on seeing someone walk quickly when there is no evident need for a fast pace, one asks why, since the walker is seen to be responding to something other than the immediate circumstance – hence not neutral.

Of course, if the walker were hurrying to avoid a falling object, then the speed would be necessary (appropriate) and therefore neutral. Walking fast when there is no need to suggests that there is an internal conflict interfering with a clear, simple response to the here and now, and so is not in accord with the universal mask. For the mask carries no conflict within it, nothing which prevents that clear, simple esponse to a stimulus.[2]*

**   Although the universal mask is not dramatic in the sense of

One can also look to the elements, to animals, and to plants for models of reacting appropriately to the present moment. Animals take from their environments what they need, when they need it, and to the extent of their needs. Emerson said that an oak or a chestnut undertakes no function it cannot execute.

One more aspect to the mask: while the actor under the universal mask is finding what is required by the situation or task at hand, the mask is drawing from him a slightly higher energy level than that of ordinary life. It is an energy held in reserve, not yet released but unmistakably there. Without it one is lacking some mask quality, some sense that the moment with mask is different from the moment without mask.

Although the universal mask takes the actor through what actor/teacher Charles Dullin called a process of depersonalization, of self-effacement before the external necessity, it is a personally enriching experience. Temporarily, and without affecting his own personality he is asked to set aside his own gestures, postures, reactions, rhythms, in order to prepare for a wider range and greater scale of character delineation to come later. Or better, he reorganizes his energies to send them flowing

---

containing conflicts that seek resolution, it can still claim a certain validity as a performing mask and apart from its value as a training tool. Dance and mime would be its natural channels, to mention only two. Marcel Marceau's sketches *The Cage* and *Youth, Maturity, Old Age and Death* could be done in a universal mask; notwithstanding his highly expressive face, the story is told in body and movement. Universal masks were used in Jacques Lecoq's mime sketch depicting the great evolutionary climb from water creatures to human beings. Myths, legends, symbol, abstraction, allegory – these would all be fitting subjects for the universal mask in performance.

through different channels, different, that is, from his own customary ones. In this way the mask enables the actor to see his own expressions of personality as elements of characterization, voluntarily used or changed at his conscious will – they are tools to draw on as soon as one is aware of them.

In spite of the depersonalization, no two people behind the same mask look alike or move alike even if they perform the same acts in a neutral, universal way. In doing simple, direct movements, devoid of personality, the mask wearer still gives an impression of being unique. It is very different from, say, a mechanical dance in which everyone looks exactly alike. In the work with the universal mask, one is not imitating a single model, but rather finding truthful, simple movements for oneself. By way of reassurance, work in the universal mask does not deny the individual, nor are human qualities stripped away. Paradoxically, by responding as would everyone else to the inherent necessities in a situation, the mask wearer is in touch with his own essence, his own inner core, the universal in him. The inner-outer harmony produces and projects a unique, larger-than-life sense of rightness belonging to that body and to no other, a sense of its participation with the things in the universe. For "he who lives in harmony with his own self lives in harmony with the universe" (Cassirer). This may sound like it goes beyond the training goals that are usually established for actors, but it serves to show why the experience of the mask is often felt to be a transcendental one.

When necessity, economy, and heightened energy all merge, the movements then have reached the mask dimension; they have nobility and grandeur, qualities that are associated with the Greek ideal of universality or with an approach to god or spirit. Walter Pater, writer on history and esthetics, might well have been speaking of a universal mask when he observed that the ancient Greek sculptors sought to "express only what is structural and permanent, to purge from the individual all that belongs only to him, all the accidents, the feelings and actions of the special moment. In this way their works came to be like some subtle extract or essence, or almost like pure thoughts or ideas; and hence the breadth of humanity in them, that detachment from the conditions of a particular place or people, which has carried their influence far beyond the age which produced them, and insured their universal acceptance."

Similar observations come from other philosophers and art critics, demonstrating the "universality" of "universal." Ernst Cassirer finds the true nature or essence of man by removing from his being all external and incidental traits. Sir Charles Bell found that the Greek sculptors studied to keep free of resemblance to any individual, giving no indication of the spirit or of the sentiments or affections; conceiving that all these movements destroy the unity of the features, and are foreign to beauty in the abstract. These are not exclusively European ideas of universality; in their carvings the African sculptors were trying to imitate not man, but God. They carved into their false faces a beauty which was not a natural beauty. In *African Masks* we find that "the artists replaced the particular by the universal which is always valid for man of every era."

However, actors working in the universal mask are not directed to play nobly or grandly. They might very well succeed if asked to do so, but would be deprived of the process of the search and its opportunity to learn something more about themselves. It would substitute an exterior quality for the inner experience. The result may look the same, but the purpose of the mask, the sensitivity and self-knowledge it can offer, would be lost. Remembering that the mask is only a tool, the actor is better served by de-emphasizing the product (to play in the dimension of mask) in favor of concentrating on finding the "other" and on discovering his/her own non-neutral elements. In that way one achieves both the process and the product too!

At times actors have asked another important question: can the universal mask be comic? The answer is no, it cannot, for reasons that have to do with the nature of comedy. One reason we laugh at the clown's movements, wrote Sigmund Freud in "Jokes and Their Relation to the Unconscious," is that they seem to us extravagant and inexpedient. We are laughing at an expenditure that is too large. But an expenditure that is too large, or too small, is on the face of it unnecessary or inadequate, both excluded by the universal mask. Further, Aristotle's definition of the ridiculous includes, in part, "what is out of time and place," but the universal reaction is one that is essential and appropriate to the time and place. Comedy often deals with failings, faults, internal conflicts – all these are alien to the universal mask. Comedy is often gamesmanship and indirect manipulation, all opposed to the simple directness of this mask. Fundamentally, the clown depends upon a certain inner contradiction in the soul of every man, wrote Enid Welsford; again, this is opposed to the mask, as are mechanical, rigid, inadaptable reactions to situations, great cause with small effect, or the reverse, or expectations not based on reality, or stumbling and falling. In fact, one could go far in devising comic effects by concentrating on such contrary, to the mask, elements of the nonessential, the uneconomical, the complex, and the indirect.

Therefore the universal mask, embodying economy, necessity, simplicity and universality, cannot at the same time contain within it the opposite features which are found in comedy. The purpose of this particular mask is not its use in a complete range of dramatic situations, but as a means for an actor to enlarge the physical aspects of his/her craft.

o o o

Actors who have worked in the universal mask have noted its effects. In the following quoted comments they speak of its freeing and enlarging qualities, but the most significant feature of their remarks is that they deal with the learning process.

> *You can forget yourself behind the mask.*
>
> *Knowing non-reality helps to know reality. Getting to the inner core is getting closer to where people are more alike.*
>
> *It's like looking at something under x-rays, stripped bare.*
>
> *It let me experience other forms of life and perception from different points of view to economize and channel energy.*
>
> *I found any move I made magnified. When I act on stage I find my body is put into more action than normal.*

It teaches me to "step out" of my own little shell, practically to melt away and to make room for a new personality. It teaches control and a tremendous amount of concentration, movements which are simple yet larger than life, and to listen to oneself as well. We all noticed our increased concentration behind the masks.

Our demonstration was the first time on stage that I didn't have stage fright.

I have always felt a bit anxious about my movements, even my physical presence on stage. Working with the mask is a unique means of stripping away extraneous movements and gestures and building selected, interpretive physical expressions.

Stage fright seemed to vanish when I put on the mask. I now feel more self-assured on stage with the mask off.

I broke through my stereotype! Everything I did was cute and young and squeaky. But not now!

In the mask you can't think ahead of what to do, you've got to stay right in this moment.

○ ○ ○

Suggested Exercises

Recommended: once the mask is on the face it is best to avoid touching it, or miming eating or drinking. The mask loses its conviction when it is confronted directly with its inability to move. If these activities are necessary, they may be covered by turning upstage or in some other way.

Exercises of everyday activities: dressing, working, preparing food. Aim: to do it simply and with no unnecessary movements.

Studies: being animals, elements, objects. Find the form, the rhythm, and the movement of each identification.

Cycle of elements: water is evaporated by sun which is hidden by clouds which are dispersed by wind which is stopped by mountain which is eroded by water.

Fantasy: excerpts from *Gulliver's Travels*; Greek, Roman, Bible myths.

Haiku poems. They can be enacted, but it is more interesting to go beyond literal interpretation into abstractions, symbols, associative meanings around the poems.

CHARACTER MASK

When characters show themselves behind masks, we must remember that character is nothing else but a mask, and that the "false face" is the true one, because it is the personal one.
– Alfred Jarry

The character mask is much easier to deal with than the universal mask, for it has reference points that are familiar to us; we all recognize elements of characterization, of comedy, personal mannerisms, internal conflict. And as would be expected, work in this mask is easier also because of the preparation offered by the universal one.

A character mask (*le masque expressif* in French) is just what the name indicates – an individual, one whose individuality is etched on the mask face. The mask bears worry lines, or a lifted corner of the mouth, or pursed lips – features that represent not a fleeting reaction but an habitual one, that has eventually created a configuration of tensed and slack muscles indelibly marking their presence on the face of one who is no longer conscious of these features.

More than a single characterization can be read into a given character mask, particularly if a mask is not designed to express one specific type of person, or emotion, or abstraction such as fear, joy, etc. (certain mask work does require such defined masks). The character masks shown in the last section are a little exaggerated from real life, and are deliberately ambiguous as to sex, state of being, or kind of person. They lend themselves to the individual actors' interpretations, as they are not confined to single personalities and can respond to an actor's projection upon them. A mask of an old, sagging face can be either a shuffling, mumbling old man, or a brisk, imperious, aging queen, among other choices. Pursed lips and concentrated gaze can suggest a compulsive, picky bookkeeper, or a kindly aunt intent on the sweater she is knitting. The importance of the work lies in developing the wearer's imaginative response to the visual stimulus of the mask, and developing an expressive body that, through identification, can fulfill the mask image physically.

The character mask is put into action in the same way as the universal mask, by reacting to the world around it, in character. In contrast to the idea of universal, the character mask brings to each moment its lifetime of experience and programming. It has learned that the world is good or bad, that life is hard or easy; it has its past experiences and its future anticipations that enter unconsciously into every transaction. It has its own internal rhythm, stance, habitual gestures, self-image; the mask comprehends quickly or slowly; it fusses over preparations for a meal or throws something together; it is fastidious or gross; the possibilities are as endless as are the number of human fancies and foibles.

On assuming a character mask, actors often try immediately to be the character. Some movements may be effective, but the mask should be given time to do its work. Better to refrain from quickly imposing gesture on the mask; better to let the mask in its own time transform into movement the image in the actor's imagination. The restraint will also help the actor to do what may at first seem like too little, for the mask amplifies everything that touches upon it. If the actor does less, the mask does more.

The same principle of identification applies as in the universal mask; the wearer feels his own features drawn into a semblance of those of the mask, and the body responds to the continuing impulse. If the actor assumes a feature of a mask such as an out-thrust chin, then continues the movement by pushing the head forward of the body, the chest may counterbalance by sinking to the back, a movement which would be completed by the pelvis tucking under. The entire body has responded to one feature of the mask, and to its own need for equilibrium.

Since the full face mask takes away from the actor the two most expressive factors, words and facial play, all expression of character, mood, situation, feeling can be revealed only through acts, gestures, pauses. Jacques Lecoq, in his Paris school of movement and theatre, employs the principle that character is revealed in the doing. Highly relevant here is Robert Benedetti's concept of Mask of Action, in which the actor is to find the specific playable action or point of reaction in each moment, expressed in simple and active ways. By their acts shall we know them: the way one stands, walks, prepares food, arranges work, gets dressed, by the looks, pauses, gestures, rhythms, actions and interactions – the infinite variety of movement of humankind is the rich vein to be mined here.

Actors unfamiliar with techniques of non-verbal communication may have a tendency to use cliches or to pantomime their actions; that is, to use the folk language of sign gestures familiar to us from ballet, or that of strangers without a common tongue, or the signals between two people on opposite sides of a noisy room (pointing for "you" or "me," hand cupping ear for "hear," etc.). To eliminate these facile "conversational" signs will push actors toward finding fresher, more interesting and profound means of making known their wishes or feelings. If a character is impatiently awaiting someone, it is too easy to communicate that fact by glancing at a watch or tapping one's foot. Instead, let an actor find other gestures, perhaps looking for long moments, or intently, in certain directions, perhaps trying not to, perhaps being unable to concentrate on something else. Such acts need to be interpreted in the specific context of the situation. They enrich the texture of characterization, and actors also become comfortable with silences, looks, immobility – in short, with a wider range of meaningful communication.

To find out as much as possible about a character it is useful to explore both its moments of drama and its moments without drama. The former may be built into the play; the latter offer opportunities for fleshing out a character. The best choices of moments to work on: when the personage is alone, doing customary, ordinary acts, in circumstances where no outside factor is exerting an influence – no sleepless night, no mood highs or lows. Essentially these are neutral acts, and here we can use the word in an extended way, useful for work in all character masks, in a

meaning slightly different from its employment with the universal mask. In this context it retains its meaning of responding to the internal necessity required by an object or situation with no dramatic content, but without the concept of the universal – that is, doing only what everyone does. For example, a character might perform some ordinary morning exercises every day, or meticulously sharpen each pencil on the desk whether it needs it or not. These acts are not universal ones, but they are neutral for the character.
It is important to find what is neutral for a character, for by living these portions of the life of that mask the body becomes imprinted with them, just as would happen in real life. These studies can give the actor the foundation for the character's dramatic moments, circumstances of pressure, and emotional interchange with others.

○   ○   ○

Comments from actors having worked in the character masks indicate some of what they found.

> *Thinking about the mask gets me into my character role in acting.*
>
> *I can assume any mask, role, now, like for an audition.*
>
> *Yesterday I didn't get anything from this mask, and today I put it on and found my face being pulled into the shape of the mask!*
>
> [After rehearsal with masks, then without]
> *We didn't mug! And didn't feel we wanted to! Because we were speaking with the body!*

The actors were cleaner, more definite, clearer with masks.

We found we went deeper into ourselves to build this tiny characterization and it happened so quickly To force yourself to move in an unusual way gets closer to the essence.

[After a workshop performance of The Lover, *rehearsed part of the time in masks] "Everything we did in masks determined what we did on stage." "The mask gave us a sense of what was dramatic – every move is amplified." "We used rhythm more – we didn't know how until we'd had mask technique." "We tended to make things small, but the mask gives a sense of importance even when you're not wearing it." "We flitted around for a long time without fixing on character, then the mask just pinpointed it." "I'm not sure when I do right but I know when I do wrong!"*

o o o

Suggested Exercises

Exercises of everyday activities of dressing, working, preparing food, and whatever a character would ordinarily do.

Sketch by Elmer Rice, *Exterior*, from his *Three Plays Without Words*, Samuel French.

Excerpts from *Alice in Wonderland,* Tolkien, etc.

Silent improvisations: groups of people in public places, like a cafe, launderette, sauna, on a bus; making no attempt to interact. Work for yourself and don't try to create drama, but don't refuse an accidental encounter, if it happens.

COUNTERMASK

*One's outer life passes in a solitude haunted
by the masks of others; one's inner life passes
in a solitude hounded by the masks of oneself.*
— Eugene O'Neill

Countermask: against the mask.

A mask, or an individual, makes a certain impression on sight. When subsequent events or closer acquaintance give the lie to that impression, when we learn that things are not always what they seem, we are in the presence of mask and countermask.

A countermask, *le contremasque* in French, is highly dramatic; it offers evident conflict between, for example, face and body, as in the combination of an open relaxed face and tensed shoulders. Or Oliver Hardy's sweet face together with his gross body. Countermask is often revealed in an act; the classic figure of the weeping clown Pagliacci also reminds one of Marcel Marceau's sketch *The Mask Maker*, whose grinning mask is belied by the body's anguished attempts to rid itself of the mask. Chaplin's sweet smiling face contrasts with the kick he is delivering. Countermask is seen in Cyrano de Bergerac's grotesque face countered by his poetic soul. The same principle can apply to two faces of a character, examples of which are a part of everyone's experience.

Usually the countermask is the first we see, and only realize later, either gradually or through a turning point in a situation, that the character behind it is not in accord with the mask. A common, real-life countermask frequently met is that of the student who gives the appearance of being over-relaxed, casual, with a low energy level, and whose every characterization includes a slouch. That particular countermask may hide resistance, nervousness, self-consciousness, lack of confidence, or boredom – it almost never reflects true relaxation. The entire body and gestures become the countermask to hide the true mask.

The idea of countermask has filled theatrical and other literature, for the switch, the exchange, the turning into something else is dramatically fascinating. Dr. Jekyl becomes Mr. Hyde, two masks of the same person. In the play *Escurial* by Ghelderode, the king and his jester exchange roles. In Pinter's *The Lover*, two people play their four (figurative) masks. Many of Pirandello's plays revolve around the idea of countermask.

The moment of change is of particular interest; what brings it about, what gestures emerge, whether gradually or suddenly, whether voluntary or not.

The undefined aspect of character masks permits them to be played as countermasks, since many personality traits can be read into them. An actor first sees a mask as a particular character, then looks for an opposite, or very different, sort of personality for the same character. A gangster can become a suave, dinner-jacketed owner of a gambling casino. A compulsive, irritable bookkeeper becomes gleeful on finding someone's error. An aging, imperious queen, once out of the public eye, is tired and worried. A performer suffers from stage fright in the dressing room, is relaxed and confident on stage.

In our time we have become aware of the many faces we wear, we all wear; the idea of countermask is fairly built into our lives, our culture. With whatever understanding we can bring to it, the countermask helps us to explore the complexities of a characterization.

o o o

To bring together the three masks discussed so far: they can be thought of as one atop the other. The universal mask is what we are, the character mask is our self-image, the countermask is the image our character presents to the world.

o o o

Suggested Exercises

Studies: play a character in some action that leads to a revealing of the mask as countermask, one mask for two aspects of the same person. Pay attention to the moment or moments of change. Variation : try with two different masks for the same person

Studies: one actor, in one mask, playing two different persons found in the same place, like a seamstress or tailor with an elegant client, or a janitor and a corporation executive in an office. Not strictly countermask, this exercise can stretch the range of mask interpretation.

Excerpts from *The Maids, The Lover. Dr. Jekyll and Mr. Hyde. Escurial.*

HALF MASK

*... behind the mask one's face is speaking,
but that's one's own secret, and the god's . .*
– Mary Renault

The half mask for training purposes seems to have been little used and less recorded, despite a certain amount of its employment on the stage, from Commedia dell'arte to avant garde and radical theatre.

Half (or three-quarter) masks are, of course, more flexible instruments than the full mask, since they permit the actor the use of the voice. What happens when the wearer is experiencing the effect of the mask, and can speak at the same time? The effect parallels that of the full mask on the body: that is, the speaker cannot use his own daily voice, cannot behave vocally as though he were not wearing a mask. It calls for a voice compatible with its heightened dimension, but what voice? In a character half mask, it will be the character voice, as in Commedia dell'arte and other kinds of productions. But with a characterless (it is tempting to call it "universal" but that might be too confusing) half mask, one can find either a neutral voice, or a character one.

The neutral voice is one that is economically placed and energized, the equivalent of the movements under the universal mask: necessary, economical, and with a mask level of energy. Such a voice can be the narrator, or the commentator, or the leader of the chorus. Actors using half masks during rehearsals of scenes from Greek plays found both the nobility of body that they had achieved in the full universal mask, and a voice that took on the same dimension.

The same neutral or characterless mask can be used in working on a role. It can help to find characterization – or perhaps it helps the actor to get out of the way so that characterization can find him – while it encourages economy and clarity. Other factors help the process: the sound of the human voice, and the strength of a text, all combine to enable the mask to give its energy and power to an actor's emerging character image. It first serves, as does the universal mask, to gear into neutral in body and voice, preparing the shift toward characterization as actors work on motivations, relationships, and text. In the half mask they attain a mask dimension of theatrical presence in both body and voice.

o o o

Actors working on scenes from *The Seagull* commented:

I felt so still, so focused, so economical all the time I was speaking the text, no wiping of hands or shifting of feet. And I got used to my partner in a mask, it never bothered me.

Did you see how I got away from my usual mixed-up-little-girl character? And I had economy!

I saw it! And you came across like a powerhouse!

Seeing them play in masks, I could see immediately when they were playing objectives or not.

Yes, I saw it too. It focused that muddy moment, made it sharper.
After, when I played without the mask, I was aware of body things, I was more self-aware. When I got off the track I knew it right away, like I knew it in the mask.

I felt more comfortable when I didn't have to worry about me, when I was masked.

Inside the mask you do the least you have to do and you know what that least is, and I get it. Out of mask I'm not sure, I don't know how much is enough, or not right away.

That's what economy feels like, you know exactly what's needed, an inevitable feeling that there's only one thing to do.

I can see the skeleton when the mask is there; I can see what's essential more than without it.

It was easier to say the words, just to say them. I was so focused.

[On voice] *Mine comes from down here, and without the mask I was aware of it coming from the same place. But no conscious shifting of gears.*

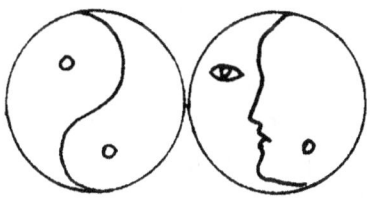

TAI CHI CH'UAN AND THE UNIVERSAL MASK

*True quiet means keeping still when the time
has come to keep still, and going forward
when the time has come to go forward.*
– I Ching Book of Changes

The orbits of the universal mask and of T'ai Chi Ch'uan intersect in several striking ways, and because they are both used in acting training programs, a discussion of what they have in common, and its relevance for the actor, is offered.

T'ai Chi Ch'uan is a Chinese health exercise, a system of contained, flowing movements (only the slow form is under present discussion) allied with a philosophy. It disciplines both mind and body; physically as the muscles learn to execute

The universal mask is a teaching tool, developed from the work of Jacques Copeau. Its aim is to help the actor to develop an expressive body, to play economically, using only essential movements, and at the heightened dimension of the mask.

the balanced, controlled motion, and mentally for the intense, unflagging concentration it requires. Its purpose, among others, is to promote mental, physical and spiritual health and well-being.

The gestures are neutral in that they are confined to the essential moves, done with the utmost economy.

Universal: necessary and economical.

The performing of each gesture is determined by the gesture itself, what Sophia Delza balls intrinsic-to-the-need energy. The wrist turns in the most economical way, with no vaiation of personal mannerisms.

The mask relates to the things in the world in their own terms; they are the "other." A tree, a rock contain their own requirements for dealing with them.

Although it is always done the same way, it is never mechanical, for the performer concentrates on the present moment as though the movements were forever new.

The mask focuses all its energies on immediate task; "every time is the first time."

In the basic stance the body is centered, straight, relaxed yet held suspended, arms hanging from the shoulders, chest neither pushed forward nor slumped. The energy level is that of readiness to move, a state of alert relaxation. The energy used is neither too much nor too little.	A universal posture is neither stiff nor limp, but lightly relaxed and potentially purposeful, ready to pickup a stone with only the necessary amount of energy.
The series of 108 forms is done slowly in an unvaried tempo. Subtle phrasing of the separate gestures, though, must be found within the unchanging tempo, mainly by being aware of beginnings, climaxes and ends of gesture phrases.	The mask calls for a tempo slower than that of non-masked real life. It fills time by investing every move with a sence of importance.
T'ai Chi calls for intense concen tration. If the mind wanders the performer becomes lost in the subtly varied repetitions of gestures. Concentrations comes easily, however, because of the slow action and the need to think about each movement. These create a deep sense	Deep concentration results from the focus on the "other," the present object or circumstance to which one is relating.

of participation and of living only in the present moment.

No emotion is expressed in T'ai Chi. Its essence is being and Chi. Its essence is being and always performed in the same way, no matter how one happens to feel. It draws the performer into a detached state, at the same time his concentration turns him inward.

Although everyone in a group does the same movements, and without personal mannerisms or style, the performers maintain their individual ways of moving.

Because of its accompanying philosophy of the yin-yang, there is no separation of spirit and body. It puts one in touch with one's center.

Emotions that would affect the direct elating to the world and what it contains are not within the function of the universal mask.

The harmony of mask, face and body produces and projects a unique, larger-than-life sense of rightness belonging to that body and to no other.

The centered, tranquil mask, through identification, calls forth a centered, tranquil body.

The face remains still, not registering any reactions. Its calmness reflects only the centered, effortless movements of the body. The concentration of body-spirit-mind, and the physical-spiritual-mental pleasure of flowing motion, bring the total being into harmony	The face under the mask assumes the mask's relaxed features, which helps to eliminate individual mannerisms. The mask gives a sense of being at one with oneself.

T'ai Chi Ch'uan touches other points of interest to the actor, apart from what it shares with the universal mask. Yin-yang concepts, the containment of opposites, can teach the inter-relatedness of things, including the interrelations of elements of characterization. Its spirit-body totality is of vital importance for the physically-mentally-spiritually integrated person. It can strengthen kinesthetic image. Its unchanging form and rhythm is like the beat and feet of verse, the construct and rhythm of text. The long, legato phrases are useful.

Suggested Exercises

Many spin off exercises, in addition to the T'ai Chi form itself, can be devised. One can mark the phrasing of the movements, inhaling with each new phrase as one would do in speaking a text. It can be done as a mirror exercise for two people . Accompanying music can dictate changing the rhythms of the movements; another challenge would consist in holding to the T'ai Chi tempo and against the music. One can do T'ai Chi letting vocal sounds emerge of themselves. Images like being under water, or threading one's way through a maze or tactile gallery, can change the movements. Nearly every variation will suggest even further exercises.

MASK AND MIME
AS
REHEARSAL AIDS

*The mechanism of the actor's process of s
elf-definition and of the dramatic
event itself is a mask of actions.*
– Robert Benedetti

In addition to using the half mask to rehearse scenes for a spoken play, another rehearsal technique is available with the full, character mask.

Cast members can choose a mask that fits the role they are playing. Even though that mask had been animated differently, as another sort of character, it can still lend itself to a new character if it sparks the actor's imagination.

With a full mask, of course, the players cannot rehearse lines. Instead, they can work on a great deal of unspoken material. The exercises suggested under character mask would be useful: finding out how the character walks, stands, and sits; how he or she gets up in the morning, dresses, prepares a meal, watches TV, feeds a child, engages in a hobby, receives a letter, or any other appropriate activities. One can choose all the times that a character is alone, or is with others in situations not requiring conversation.

Then there are circumstances related to the play but not included in the script. What does the character do a few minutes before an entrance? After an exit? While off stage?

A mask is not required in order to do these rehearsal exercises; directors have been using them for a long time. A mask, however, helps to focus energies and heighten dramatic intensity; it constantly reminds the wearer of the non-verbal, therefore physical, aspect of his work.

Still another technique can be used to deepen and strengthen the actor's understanding of his role and his objectives. A given scene can be translated into a series of physical acts, paralleling the motivations in the text; by playing such a physical enactment actors are helped to focus on what their characters are about at that moment. These equivalent gestures (equivalent to what the character wants) become a metaphor of the intentions contained in the scene. It is a mimed version of the text, it is text committed to gesture. Here one is working not from character so much as from text; text is the "other."

Important: as is mentioned earlier, actors should avoid simply pantomiming in sign language; such gestures are not metaphors, but substitutes for words, and not productive for this purpose. Example: to pantomime a love scene one would do the familiar hand-heart-offering gestures, or variations of them. Metaphorical gesture might consist of standing close together, or looking at each other, or taking hands, or touching. Perhaps this is body language too. Whatever it is called, it is a rich area of mask work. Just as the mask does in the workshop studies, it will perform its task of determining the essential, economical movements. It will also create the larger-than-life dimension that some directors will look for. If that dimension is desired, actors should use masks until its lessons are established in the body; the length of time will vary with different people. And the director can always bring back some mask work at any time during rehearsals or runs, even for brief improvisations.

BIBLIOGRAPHY

Very little has been written in English, only slightly more in French, on the mask as it affects the actor. Many of the references below are from the fields of anthropology, sociology, theatre history, art, and psychology, included here for their relevant sections.

List of Works Consulted

John Arden interview, Marowitz and Trussler, *Theatre at Work*

Wallace A. Bacon and Robert S. Breen, *Literature as Experience*

Sir Charles Bell, *The Anatomy and Philosophy of Expression*

Robert Benedetti, "The Mask of Actions," *Actor Training 1*, Richard P. Brown, Ed.

Ernest Cassirer, *An Essay on Man*

Leon Chancerel, preface to *La Farce du Chaudronnier*

Michael Chekhov, *To the Actor*

Michael Chekhov, *To the Director and Playwright*
Jean Cocteau, preface to "Le Boeuf sur le Toit," *The Drama Review* (T-55) September 1972

Denarius Deane, "Maker of Tragic Masks," source unknown

Sophia Delza, "The Exercise Art of T'ai Chi Ch'uan," *Drama and Theatre*, Fall 1969

Jean Dorcy, *The Mime*

Jean Dorcy, *J'Aime la Mime*

Charles Dullin, *Souvenirs et notes de travail d'un acteur*

Sears A. Eldredge, "Masks: Their Use and Effectiveness in Actor Training Programs," doctoral dissertation Michigan State University, 1975

Sigmund Freud, 'Jokes and Their Relation to the Unconscious,' *Theories of Comedy*, John Lauter, Ed.

Richard Goodwin interview on the film "Peter Rabbit and Tales of Beatrix Potter," source unknown

Kenneth Macgowan, "Masks and Their Meaning," *International Studio*, November 1923

Margaret Mead, "Masks and Man," *Natural History* LV #6, June 1946

Franco Monti, *African Masks*
Eugene O'Neill, "Memoranda on Masks," *Playwrights on Playwriting*
Walter F. Otto, *Dionysus, Myth and Cult*

Alessandro Pizzorno, "Le Masque," *Cahiers Renaud-Barrault* #31 (anthropology)

Bari Rolfe, "The Actor's World of Silence," *Quarterly Journal of Speech*, December 1969

Bari Rolfe, "The Mime of Jacques Lecoq," *The Drama Review* (T-53) March 1972

Michel Saint-Denis, *Theatre: The Rediscovery of style*

Peter Schumann interview, in Eldredge

Harry Shapiro, catalog notes on masks, American Museum of Natural History

Mary Wigman, *The Language of Dance*

Charlotte Wolff, "The Nature of Gesture, *The Psychology of Gesture*

Other Useful Works

Gustav Attinger, *L'Esprit de la commedia dell'arte dans le theatre français*

J. L. Bedouin, *Les Masques* (anthropology)
W. T. Benda, *Masks* (art objects)

Oto Bihalji-Merin, *Great Masks* (history, anthropology, sociology, art, drama)

Georges Buraud, *Les Masques* (anthropology)

Jarka Burian, "Otomar Krejca's Use of the Mask," *The Drama Review* (T-55), September 1972

Joseph Campbell, "The Lesson of the Mask," *The Masks of God*, Vol. 1 (mythology)

Leon Chancerel, *Le Masque* (theatre history)

Jan Doat, *L'Expression corporelle du comedien*

P. L. Duchartre, *The Italian Comedy*

Josef Gregor, *Masks of the World* (history, anthropology)
Eleanor King, "The Magic of Masks," *Dance Magazine*, August 1963 (Eastern, Western dance theatre)

E. T. Kirby, "The Mask: Abstract Theatre, Primitive and Modern," *The Drama Review* (T-55) September 1972

V. Meyerhold, "The Fairground Booth," *Meyerhold on*

Theatre, Edward T. Braun, Ed. Also translated as "Farce," *Theatre in the Twentieth Century*, Robert Corrigan, Ed.

Mime Journal Number Two, June 1975 (issue on masks)

Allardyce Nicoll, *Masks, Mimes and Miracles*

Mary Renault, *The Mask of Apollo* (novel)

Jamie Shalleck, *Masks* (real life masks)

PHOTOGRAPHS

Half Mask, 66

Universal Mask, 67

Character Masks, 68 - 69

Masks in rehearsals and workshops, 70 - 77

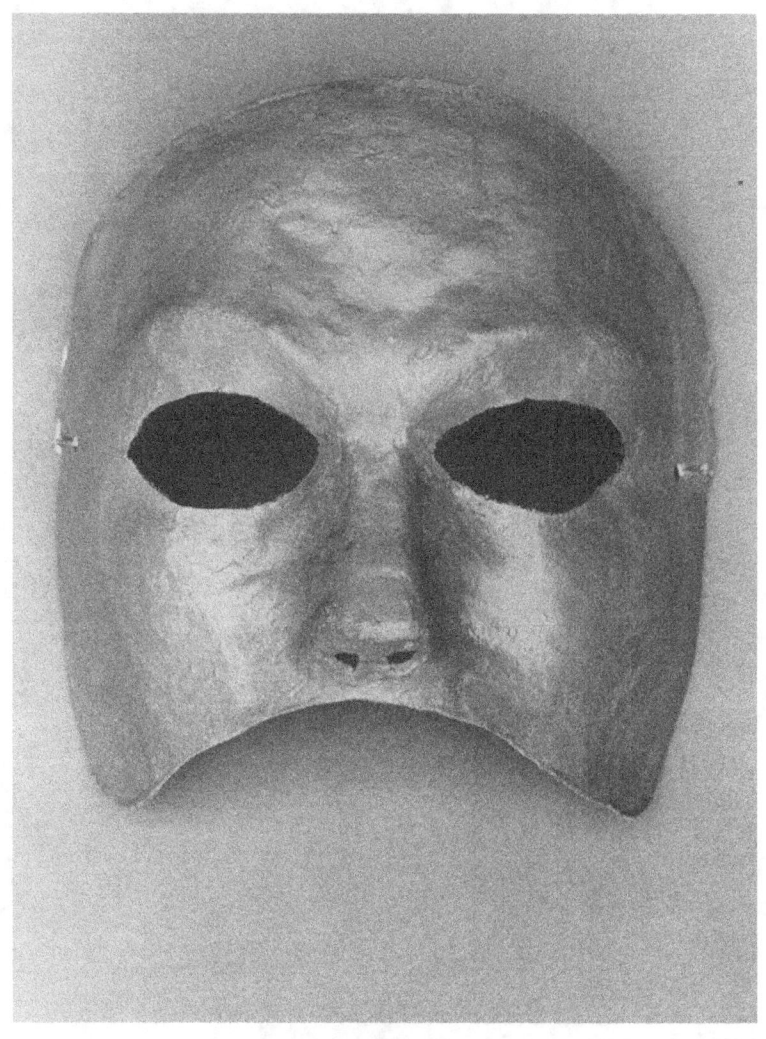

Half Mask

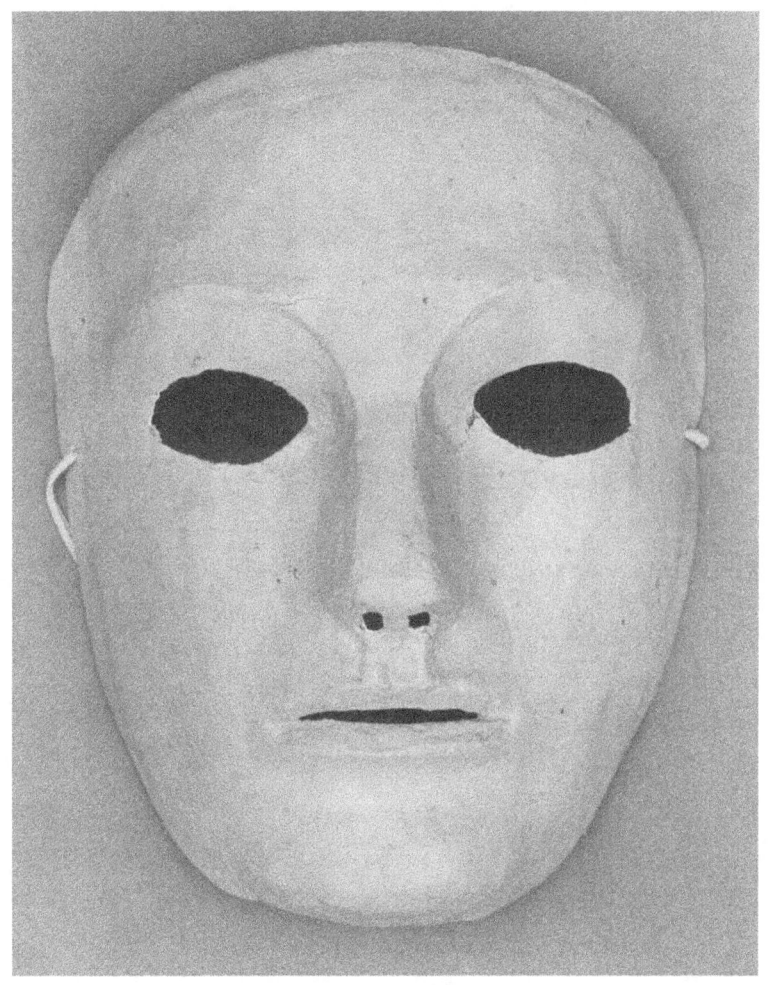

Universal Mask

Character Masks

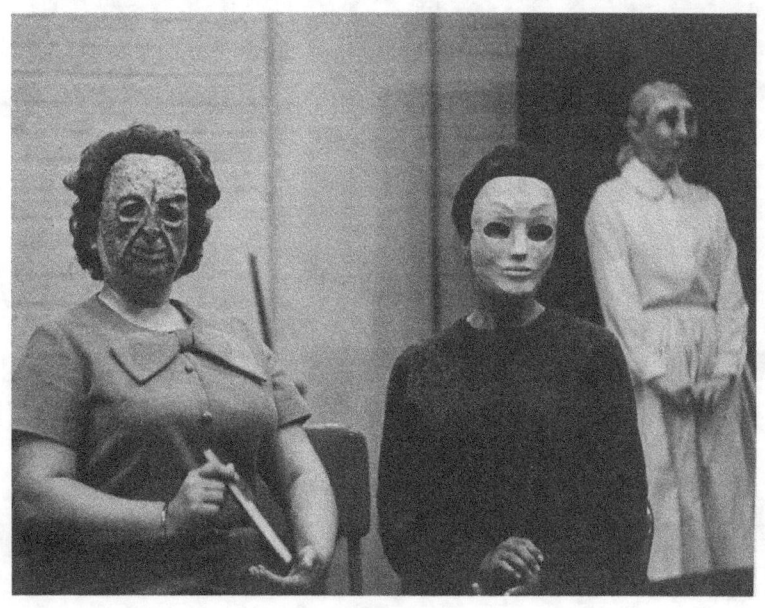

www.ingramcontent.com/pod-product-compliance
Lightning Source LLC
Chambersburg PA
CBHW050605300426
44112CB00013B/2087